Praise

"Prayer for a follower of Christ is slowing down to take a deep breath of the things of our Lord. Unfortunately, most Christians today are oxygen deprived. *Prayers from the Pews* beckons us back to seeking and seeing our Father's face by using the book of Acts to pray for our local churches. Teri literally has invited us to breathe again!"

MICHAEL MOHLER
Pastor, Trinity Point Church
South Carolina Baptist Convention Discipleship Coordinator

"Teri Lynne Underwood has nailed my heart in her book, *Prayers from the Pews*. I've been guilty of criticizing church, and many times I've asked the church to change when it was really my own heart that needed work. *Prayers from the Pews* is a call to action not for The Church, but for the church—those of us who grace the pews (or chairs, or couch, or kitchen stools)—to get on our knees and beg God to change our hearts, turning them toward His Word, and choosing to humble ourselves and love others more than ourselves. I highly recommend it."

BROOKE MCGLOTHLIN
www.brookemcglothlin.com
Author, *Warrior Prayers* and *Hope for the Weary Mom*

"*Prayers from the Pews* is an excellent book on how to pray in a practical way. Often times we pray general prayers for our church, for ourselves, and for others. *Prayers from the Pews* shows us how to really pray! Teri Lynne gives you a honest look at the church and how we can pray for the church, for our leaders, for others and for ourselves. The prayer guides and the book of Acts reading plan are great devotional tools that will help you in your daily worship of God. I highly recommend this book to everyone as it will help you learn to pray."

LEE PEOPLES
Pastor, Stewartstown Baptist Church

"With so much negative rhetoric being tossed around about the Church these days, Teri Lynne Underwood shares a refreshing, encouraging, and very welcome message in her new book, *Prayers from the Pews*. Going straight to the Bible, Teri Lynne offers the solution to much of today's dissatisfaction with the church – prayer. But Teri Lynne doesn't simply suggest we pray, she give us solid guidance and 30 heart-felt, biblically-based prayers to offer up for our churches. *Prayers from the Pews* is a practical tool that also delivers insight about prayer, worship, and revival."

KATHY HOWARD
www.kathyhoward.org
Author, *Unshakeable Faith, Before His Throne,* and *God's Truth Revealed*

Prayers from the Pews

THE POWER OF PRAYING FOR YOUR CHURCH

Teri Lynne Underwood

4

© 2012 by Teri Lynne Underwood

All rights reserved. No portion of this book may be reproduced, stored in a retrieval system, or transmitted in any form or by any means—electronic, mechanical, photocopy, recording, scanning, or other—except for brief quotations in critical reviews or articles without the prior written permission of the author.

ISBN 978-1478153634

Edited by Sandra Peoples of Next Step Editing.
www.nextstepediting.com
Cover design and layout by Phil Ulrich of Design By Insight.
www.designbyinsight.net
Cover image via iStock Photo.
Author photography by His and Hers Photography.
www.hisandhersphtoography.com

All Scripture quotations, unless otherwise indicated, are taken from The Holy Bible, English Standard Version®, ESV®. Copyright © 2001 by Crossway, a publishing ministry of Good News Publishers. Used by permission. All rights reserved.

Scripture quotations marked NIV are from The Holy Bible, New International Version®, NIV®. Copyright © 1973, 1978, 1984, 2011 by Biblica, Inc.™ Used by permission. All rights reserved.

Scripture quotations marked NASB are taken from the *New American Standard Bible*. Copyright © 1960, 1962, 1963, 1968, 1971, 1972, 1973, 1975, 1977, 1995 by The Lockman Foundation. Used by permission.

For Scott

Thank you for pushing me to share my heart on this topic, for being patient when I was ready to give up on the church, and for loving me the way Christ loves His bride.

Table of Contents

INTRODUCTION . . . 17

WHY PRAY . . . 21

I'M JUST NOT SURE ABOUT THE CHURCH SOMETIMES . . . 25

THE WEAKEST LINK . . . 31

RE-LIFE . . . 37

THE PERFECT CHURCH . . . 45

THE PROBLEM WITH CHURCH . . . 51

WELL DONE OR WELL SAID . . . 57

CHRIST IS PROCLAIMED . . . 63

THE NECESSITY OF SILENCE . . . 69

PARTAKERS OF GRACE . . . 73

THIRTY PRAYERS FOR YOUR CHURCH . . . 79

PRAYERS FOR THE HEART OF YOUR CHURCH . . . 81

PRAYERS FOR THE MINISTRY OF YOUR CHURCH . . . 95

PRAYERS FOR YOUR PASTORS . . . 105

PRAYERS FOR YOURSELF AND FELLOW BELIEVERS . . . 113

READING PLAN FOR THE BOOK OF ACTS . . . 123

DISCUSSION QUESTIONS . . . 127

NOTES . . . 133

ACKNOWLEDGEMENTS . . . 135

ABOUT THE AUTHOR . . . 139

16

Introduction

The doors open as the organ rings out those familiar first notes of the "Wedding March," all eyes on the bride as she carefully and slowly begins her journey down the aisle.

Her father looks at her with misty eyes, thinking he never thought this day would really come, and that she has never been so beautiful. The bride takes steady steps toward her groom, this one to whom she is ready to pledge her life, her heart, her all.

As she arrives at the front of the church, the minister solemnly asks, "Who gives this woman to wed this man?" Every daddy in the room swallows deep as the bride's father utters, through his choked up emotions, "Her mother and I do." He leans over to kiss her and gently places this hand he has loved since he first counted every one of the ten little fingers in a hospital room into the hand of the man who will now bear the burden of caring for and providing for and loving wholly and holy his little girl.

Honestly, for most of us, this is the first moment we notice the groom. As he looks at this woman, his bride, the one who said, "Yes" to his invitation of a life lived as one, we see the most beautiful picture of Jesus.

Time and again in Scripture we see the metaphor of the church being a bride and our relationship with God reflecting marriage. In fact, Paul says marriage represents the great mystery of God's love for those who are called according to His name.

It's been said every bride is beautiful, and most especially every bride is beautiful to her groom. Imagine how beautiful the church is to Christ. He has promised His Bride He will come again and that we will spend eternity together. Christ loves His Bride! He has gone to prepare a place for her, for us...where we will be together forever.

<u>Maybe it's time we looked at the Church the way Jesus does, as the beautiful Bride.</u>

What follows is my journey—a collection of thoughts and understandings about the church and our responsibility to and as the Bride of Christ. In addition, you will find a prayer guide based on the Book of Acts that uses verses from the biblical account of the first church as a basis for 30 specific prayers for our churches, our pastors, and ourselves. Finally, because all authority comes from the Word, I've created a 40-day reading guide for you to read through Acts.

My prayer is simply this: as we read the Word, pray the Word, and meditate on the Word, God will change each of us. And as He changes each part of the Body, the Body itself will also be changed…to His glory and for His honor.

Join me?

Why Pray?

I am a believer in the salvation brought by the Lord Jesus Christ. I believe He is the only way to eternal life, that I can never be good enough or do enough to tip the scales in my favor.

But I fail . . . every. single. day. I rush through life missing the blessings of the small. I neglect the call to be still. I fail to reach out to those in need. I'm a sinner—a big one!—in desperate need of grace and mercy and forgiveness. I often think if others could see inside my heart they would run as hard and fast in the other direction as possible. I'm not perfect, I'm not good . . . most days, I could best be described as "a mess."

I am a church member and a pastor's wife.

I love my church . . . as imperfect as it is.

Is "the church" all it could or should be? Nope! It's made up of people just like me . . . imperfect, selfish, and demanding. But does that mean we don't need it? That we should toss it to the side? I find that hard to accept. Maybe it's because as a pastor's wife, daughter, granddaughter, great-granddaughter, and sister I've seen too much from the other side. I've seen the hours spent preparing for sermons and services, the all-night vigils with families in grief, the days when all plans get tossed aside because of another family's urgent need. I've seen the hurt on faces of men and women who have given their lives to minister to others and found nothing but criticism.

But I've also seen a glimpse of what heaven might be—a sanctuary filled with people of all ages and races, hands lifted high praising the living God.

And I wonder if we all spent more time digging deep into ourselves, opening up our own hearts to what the Lord is saying, acknowledging our own failures and desperate need for grace, if just maybe our churches would be a little bit different.

This tome is the result of my own soul-searching and Scripture-digging on this topic of the church. More and more I've become convinced of one thing: prayer is the key.

Prayers of gratitude for a faith family who gives generously and sacrificially to meet needs in our community and around the world.

Prayers for the wisdom and protection for our leadership.

6/23/15

Prayers for honesty and integrity among our members.

8/20/15

Prayers for healing and restoration.

Unity —

Because the answer to this question of finding the right church isn't in starting a new one, the answer—the only answer—is prayer. Fervent prayer that availeth much[1] . . . prayers for ourselves and for our churches.

Prayer from the Pew:

Lord, teach me the need for prayer. Not just the shallow, trite mumblings of "bless my church," but rather the urgent longing to see Your Bride reflect the glory of You. Cause me to be desperate to intercede on her behalf. Open my eyes to the beauty of this gift of faith family and train my heart to be ever thankful to be a part of what You are doing here on earth. In Your Son's name, Amen.

I'm Just Not Sure about The Church Sometimes

> **SINCE THE DAYS OF PENTECOST, HAS THE WHOLE CHURCH EVER PUT ASIDE EVERY OTHER WORK AND WAITED UPON HIM FOR TEN DAYS, THAT THE SPIRIT'S POWER MIGHT BE MANIFESTED? WE GIVE TOO MUCH ATTENTION TO THE METHOD AND MACHINERY AND RESOURCES, AND TOO LITTLE TO THE SOURCE OF THE POWER.**
>
> HUDSON TAYLOR

I am not always sure about the church . . . not The Church, as in the Body of Christ, but the "little c" church. Truth be told, I love being a part of a home group and feel like it represents the very best of what a local faith family ought to be. In fact, since we left our last church (my husband is a minister and we were called to a different church), it has been my home group I miss the most, followed closely by the small group of ladies I was privileged to mentor over the ten years we served there.

We crave fellowship and intimacy with one another. That can be hard to find in a sanctuary where, if Billy Graham is correct, 80% of those in attendance are unsaved, We crave authenticity and accountability. Those two things seem next to impossible to find in many local churches. I have a long list of reasons why, but most of them boil down to pride and its evil twin insecurity.

Like the vast majority of people in my small southern community, every Sunday I get dressed for church, grab my Bible, fuss at my child in the car, pull into the church parking lot, and plaster on my Sunday smile . . . I'm all ready for worship.

Only I'm not. And, the truth is, the more I talk to others and the more I read what other people write, I realize I'm not alone. In fact, I'm in the large majority.

What makes the 21st century church a place where people go for connection and leave feeling even more alone? Why are we losing a whole generation who find attending, and especially joining, a church to be a waste of time? What is the difference between the modern church and the first century church?

Some would argue it is the machinery of the modern church. Others would claim the mass marketing of Jesus stuff is the culprit. And still others would say the mega-church mindset is the root of the problem.

Today many are calling for a return to the basics of the early church. Home churches and church plants abound—a vast majority of them promising to be the "church for people who don't like church."

All of this has raised legitimate questions about topics such as the size of our churches or the need for paid staff. There have been moments I have questioned if the institution of the church has destroyed the Bride of Christ. While countless people who are more educated, more articulate, and certainly more outspoken than I am have written volumes on the topic of what's wrong with the church, I found many of those books, articles, and blog posts to be contributors to the problem rather than seekers of a solution.

In fact, I finally reached the point where I just quit reading. Not because I didn't believe the church has its failings. Not because I didn't understand how much harm and abuse has been done by leadership of the church. Not because I didn't recognize there was truth in the midst of the writing.

No, I quit reading because I became convinced we were asking the wrong questions. All the questions seemed to be about "me." I don't think it matters one lick to God where we meet—house, cathedral, or grove of trees. Because Scripture is clear:

> FOR WHERE TWO OR THREE HAVE GATHERED TOGETHER IN MY NAME, THERE I AM IN THEIR MIDST.
> MATTHEW 18:20

The issue isn't where we gather—it's why we gather.

> AND HE SAID TO THEM, "IT IS WRITTEN, 'MY HOUSE SHALL BE CALLED A HOUSE OF PRAYER.'"
> MATTHEW 21:13A

The problem isn't too many programs—it's too little prayer.

As I began wrapping my heart around the Word and seeking wisdom from Scripture (not giving my attention to the writings of others), I found time and again that God has very specific desires for those gathered in His name. We have clear instruction about His plan for the Church. While many things in Scripture can be elusive, the truth that God intends us to worship, serve, and fellowship together is not one of them.

That "together" must begin with prayer: prayer for the Church, for our churches, for pastors and leaders, and for ourselves.

This book is a tool, a starting point for exploring this noble mission of praying for our churches. I'm not a theologian or Bible scholar. I am a believer—a messed up, falling down, failing constantly, clinging to grace believer. I believe God's Word gives us the direction we need in all things. We must begin by studying Scripture to find the way to praying for the Bride of Christ.

Prayer from the Pew:

Sometimes, Lord, it must break Your heart to look down at Your kids. Bickering, back-biting, blaming. So focused on their own desires that they, WE!, miss the beauty of experiencing You. Will you grant me a tender heart for Your church? Give me a compassion for Your children and a desire to walk beside others on this disciple's journey. For all the times I've missed the point, Lord, I am sorry. Teach me, train me. In Jesus' name, Amen.

The Weakest Link

> **ONE HUNDRED RELIGIOUS PERSONS KNIT INTO A UNITY BY CAREFUL ORGANIZATION DO NOT CONSTITUTE A CHURCH ANY MORE THAN ELEVEN DEAD MEN MAKE A FOOTBALL TEAM. THE FIRST REQUISITE IS LIFE, ALWAYS.**
>
> A. W. TOZER

I need to admit something up front: I've been the problem in church. I often cry when I read about the many wounds inflicted by church people who have never quite managed to grasp the love of Christ and show it to others. Because I've been the one who hurt others.

I've been accused of being aloof, stuck up, stand-offish. I've been told I don't really care about people and I'm too busy for others. I've been told I'm the reason people have left our church and I'm the reason people haven't come back.

And my heart hurts. In fact, it aches.

I don't ever want to hurt someone, to offend someone. I'd never intentionally exclude someone from ministry or cause someone to feel unwelcome at our church. But I have, and coming to grips with that has been difficult.

It's changed me. Made me more cautious. In fact, I've become the very things that I was accused of being. I find myself being less social, less open, less likely to reach out. Because if reaching out leads to being misunderstood and leads to being hurt, then it's so much easier to sit back and say nothing. To hide . . . to smile a fake smile at everyone and develop relationships with no one.

<u>But the Lord is working. He's healing me, soothing me with the balm of His Word. I find comfort in passages like these:</u>

> ✷ But now thus says the Lord, He who created you, O Jacob, He who formed you, O Israel: "Fear not, for I have redeemed you; **I have called you by name, you are Mine.** When you pass through the waters, I will be with you; and through the rivers, they shall not overwhelm you; when you walk through the fire you shall not be burned, and the flame shall not consume you . . . **Because you are precious in My eyes, and honored, and I love you.**"
>
> Isaiah 43:1-2, 4 emphasis added

The point isn't what others think of me . . . though I have made some sincere apologies and tried to change some behaviors that have consistently seemed to hurt people. The point is I belong to the LORD. I am HIS! I am precious to Him. He loves me.

Maybe you are one of those people who has been hurt by someone who claimed the name of Christ; I can relate. Maybe you've hurt someone in your church; I can relate. Maybe you have no idea what I'm talking about; I can't relate but I am thankful for you.

Regardless, the truth is simple . . . we're going to get hurt and we're going to hurt others. It's just going to happen. We live in this fallen world and that's part of the price.

The key is this:

> WE LOVE BECAUSE **HE** FIRST LOVED US.
> 1 JOHN 4:19 EMPHASIS ADDED

And so, because of that love we are called to love others.

> BELOVED, IF GOD SO LOVED US, WE ALSO OUGHT TO LOVE ONE ANOTHER.
> 1 JOHN 4:11

The truth is any one of us could be the weak link in the church chain at any given time. We're flawed, sinful, wretched, and selfish. I've heard it said, "Wounded people wound people." If that's true, our churches are full to the brim with the wounded.

Before we go any further, I encourage you to invite God to search your heart. Perhaps you need to spend some time in prayer. Maybe you have a relationship that needs to be mended. You may need to forgive someone and allow the Great Physician to heal some old wounds. The church—local and global—needs believers who are repentant and willing to both extend and receive grace.

Prayer from the Pew:

Father, search my heart and lead me to repentance. Give me a fresh understanding of the love You have for me, so I may understand anew the love I must offer others. I pray, O God, that Your love will stir in me and heal the wounds. Cause me, Father, to be a vessel of reconciliation and of grace in my faith family. In Jesus' name, Amen.

Re-Life

BEING A CHRISTIAN IS MORE THAN JUST AN INSTANTANEOUS CONVERSION—IT IS A DAILY PROCESS WHEREBY YOU GROW TO BE MORE AND MORE LIKE CHRIST.

BILLY GRAHAM

I'm a Southern Baptist who happily lives in the Deep South. We do two things very well: fry chicken and plan a revival. Most of my life I've attended both fall and spring revivals at whatever church I was attending. I know all about revivals.

Unfortunately, my expertise in revival meetings has not always translated into a sincere spiritual, personal revival. In order for us to experience the results of praying for our churches, we need to begin with personal revival in our own hearts. While the word "revival" is not used in the New Testament, the concept of revival is key to all the early church experienced.

Revival, in the Greek, is the word *anazao*[2], meaning "to recover life." Isn't that what so many of us need: to recover the life we have received through Christ?

> THE THIEF COMES ONLY TO STEAL, AND KILL, AND DESTROY; I CAME THAT THEY MIGHT HAVE LIFE, AND MIGHT HAVE IT ABUNDANTLY.
> JOHN 10:10

Far too often, what is missing in the life of Christians is the abundance we have been promised by Christ. We need to recover the life He has given us.

Experiencing that re-life involves three principles.

REPENTANCE ALWAYS PRECEDES REVIVAL.

We cannot live in the abundant life God has for us when we are clinging to the things of this world. Repentance is the necessary precursor to true revival—individually and corporately. It's also the part we like least. It's hard work, this coming clean before God. And we resist the call to turn from our sin.

We must come to understand that confessing and forsaking the sinful patterns of this world are not optional for the believer who yearns for intimacy with Christ. The writer of Romans tells us:

> AND DO NOT BE CONFORMED TO THIS WORLD, BUT BE TRANSFORMED BY THE RENEWING OF YOUR MIND, THAT YOU MAY PROVE WHAT THE WILL OF GOD IS, THAT WHICH IS GOOD AND ACCEPTABLE AND PERFECT.
> ROMANS 12:2

As we are transformed by the Word of God, conviction will come, and as we are faithful to lay aside "the sin which so easily entangles us[3]," we find that experiencing personal renewal and revival comes far more often and easily.

REVIVAL RESTS ON THE PROCLAMATION OF THE WORD OF GOD.

We cannot initiate revival, in our own hearts nor in our churches. We can plan meetings, do Bible studies, attend prayer meetings, participate in fasts, and organize events, but we cannot manufacture re-life. Only God can breathe life time and again into the hearts of those who seek Him.

Then the Lord God formed man of dust from the ground, and breathed into his nostrils the breath of life; and man became a living being.
Genesis 3:7

The Spirit of God has made me, and the breath of the Almighty gives me life.
Job 33:4

Jesus said to him, "I am the way, and the truth, and the life; no one comes to the Father, but through Me."
John 14:6

Life comes from God alone and our lives are revived, recovered, through time spent in the Word. God's Word is spoken to us through the pages of our Bibles just as surely as it was spoken to the men who were inspired by Him to pen the original manuscripts. His Word is life to us. True revival requires we engage with Scripture and apply what we learn.

Revival results in genuine worship.

It happens all the time. We attend a series of meetings, listen to dynamic preaching, hear moving music, and come away believing we have had revival. We are emotionally connected to the experience, but far too often we are not spiritually changed by an encounter with God.

Jesus explained to the woman at the well that the time would come when we would worship in spirit and in truth. True worship is not merely an emotional reaction to external circumstances; true worship leads us beyond the emotion and experience into a deeper realization of the nature and character of God.

When churches—and individuals—are re-lifed, revived, we are changed from the inside out. Our experiences reflect our intimacy with Christ. Our worship moves beyond lyric and melody and is manifested in service and humility.

Genuine worship has nothing to do with the mode or method of the worshipper; it is entirely devoted to pleasing the Object of our worship.

Maybe you realize you need *anazao*—your life needs to be recovered. I invite you to slow down today and ask the Holy Spirit to work in you, to lead you to genuine worship.

Prayer from the Pew:

I need some re-life, Lord. I'm weary and worn. Will You recover me? Recover the life You have given me and teach me the beauty of true worship, true relationship. Cause my heart to see only You, be devoted only to You. As I am revived, I pray You will receive glory and draw others to You and the life only You can give. In Jesus' name, Amen.

The Perfect Church

> **THE PERFECT CHURCH SERVICE WOULD BE ONE WE WERE ALMOST UNAWARE OF. OUR ATTENTION WOULD HAVE BEEN ON GOD.**
>
> C. S. LEWIS

What is wrong with your church? With the church?
If you are like most people I know, you could make a list a mile long of ways the church globally and locally could be doing a better job, should be doing a better job.

Most of us figure we could do a better job of leading and decision-making than the leaders and decision-makers do. Maybe we are right.

The thing is I'm just not sure that's where our energy should be focused.

I've been contemplating "the perfect church" lately. What would it have? What would it NOT have? Here are a few of the things I came up with to characterize the perfect church:

- A church that is Bible-teaching, unapologetic for the hard doctrines but grace-filled in dealing with the ever-failing members of its body.
- A church that values women, that embraces our obligation to those in need, that esteems the widows and takes care of the elderly.
- A church that values creativity in all its forms (dancing, painting, singing, writing, graphics, etc.).
- A church that studies the Word, not one that relies on the easiest, cheapest curriculum, that has teachers who are passionate and invested in the spiritual formation of their classes.
- A church that prays—often, regularly, spontaneously, and openly.
- A church that uses Bible words like "sin" rather than the more palatable "mistake."
- A church that expects me to be accountable for my spiritual gifting, my finances, my attributes, my testimony.

But the reality is, that church only exists in my mind. Oh sure, some of those things may be true most of the time and most may occur some of the time, but none of them happen all the time. Not because our leadership is lazy . . . nor because our congregation doesn't care. Honestly, it's because I don't live that way.

When I read over that list of what I want the perfect church to be, I realized it is really a list of what I believe God has called me to be. That list represents the convictions He has placed on my heart over the past 18 years of purposing to live for Him.

The truth is, my church can never be what God has called ME to be. Getting that distinction straight has taken me a while.

When I am burdened or my eyes opened to an issue or situation, that is not so I can send an email to my family deacon to alert him of the need . . . it's so I can act.

I'm discovering that much of the dissatisfaction with "church" could really be the Lord trying to reveal the layers of apathy and fear in our own lives.

The simple reality is this: I am guilty. I've been critical and pulled away from the Bride of Christ. Because, for me, it's just always easier to be right than to be righteous. I want things done my way, the way that seems best to me, the way that makes sense to me.

And that's not just true in regard to church, I see it revealed in every area of my life. The question I've asked myself and I'd ask you too is, "What makes a perfect church to you?" And then, "What are you doing to make those qualities reality in your own life?"

Prayer from the Pew:

This one is hard, God. It's hard to admit the depths of my selfishness, the width of my pride, the height of my stubbornness. But there they are, on display for all to see. Forgive me, Father, for the way I've tried to make the church into something it was never intended to be. Will You, Lord, work in me? Will You help me see the disciple You want me to be? And as I become that person, then I can fill the role, become the part of the Body, for which You created me. In Jesus' name, Amen.

The Problem with Church

THE CHURCH IS NOT A GALLERY FOR THE BETTER EXHIBITION OF EMINENT CHRISTIANS, BUT A SCHOOL FOR THE EDUCATION OF IMPERFECT ONES.

HENRY WARD BEECHER

All this contemplation has led me to realize that <u>maybe, just maybe, the problem with the church is me</u>. Well, maybe not the whole problem . . . but <u>at least part of the problem.</u>

<u>I come to church with these expectations and wounds and desires. So</u> do you, I bet. And when those expectations are not met, when those wounds are reopened, when those desires are not realized, well, I don't like it.

IN NO WAY AM I ATTEMPTING TO MINIMIZE THE LEGITIMATE HURTS AND ABUSE THAT HAVE BEEN CAUSED BY AND IN CHURCHES.

I would never want to imply or infer that the wounding experienced by many (many!) of my friends at the hands of church leaders and misappropriated Scripture is small or somehow not real. It is real. And it breaks my heart—just as I firmly believe it breaks the heart of God.

But that is not what I'm referring to here. Aside from unbiblical teaching or immoral action among church leadership, I wonder how much of the issue with the "institution of church" is rooted in self? I am not implying that all who have left larger churches and moved to a smaller, more organic model of corporate worship are selfish . . . I don't believe that at all. I have precious, godly friends who have been led to plant churches.

<u>I firmly believe we must bathe all decisions in deep prayer, willing to follow the Lord's direction—whether it lines up with our own desires or not.</u>

A few years ago I was struggling with my church and the way I felt about "church" in general. We'd been through some difficult seasons and I had reached a point of wanting to throw in the towel. I'd felt the stones of judgment hit hard against my flesh and I'd seen the seeds of bitterness and entitlement flourish in an environment of "me-centered worship." To be honest, I was ready to walk away from all of it . . . and, at one point, I even told my husband I wanted him to leave the ministry.

I'd been hurt badly. Words spoken to me and about me left deep holes of doubt in the fabric of my faith. Rejection by people who did not even know me burned hot inside my heart.

That's all to say, I know what "church people" can be. In the words of the old farmer, "I are one." I've been hurt and I've been the one who did the hurting.

But when I was ready to give up on the church, walk away from this body that punched itself and refused to be honest about the wounds, I read this little piece of Scripture and it stopped me cold.

> Do nothing from rivalry or conceit, but in humility count others more significant than yourselves. Let each of you look not only to his own interests, but also to the interests of others.
>
> Philippians 2:3-4

Sometimes I am competitive. Sometimes I can be conceited and prideful. Humility doesn't come natural and I am often guilty of elevating my interests (my preferences?) over those of others. And yet somehow I seem to forget that those attitudes, those behaviors, affect the tone of my church, the heart of my church.

This business of being a part of the church, it's tough stuff. And when I have to look at my heart, I realize it can be pretty hard too.

Prayer from the Pew:

Jesus, You are the picture of humility. You gave up heaven and all its glory for this dusty, broken world. You left behind the honor and power that was rightfully Yours for a trip to the cross. Me? I don't even want to sing songs I don't like. And I sure don't want to choose to be less so others can be more. I miss the point most of the time, don't I? Will you teach me to grasp that when I make myself less it's not those around me who become more, it's You. All You. Cause me to find contentment there in that place of smallness before Your greatness. In Jesus' name, Amen.

Well Done or Well Said

> **CHURCH ISN'T WHERE YOU MEET. CHURCH ISN'T A BUILDING. CHURCH IS WHAT YOU DO. CHURCH IS WHO YOU ARE. CHURCH IS THE HUMAN NETWORKING OF THE PERSON OF JESUS CHRIST. LET'S NOT GO TO CHURCH, LET'S BE THE CHURCH.**
>
> BRIDGET WILLARD

I recently read *7: An Experimental Mutiny Against Excess* by Jen Hatmaker. Wow! {If you haven't read it, do!} Sometimes a book forces me to rethink my positions, my rationalizations, my thoughts about what I "know." This book is one of them. While I was reading Jen's book, I was writing a lot about the church on my blog. In fact, a large portion of this book is an expansion of the ideas I began to flesh there.

Questions like: Is there a place for the "institutional church"? Are we really doing anything Jesus would do? Would He have rejected joining with my church and instead formed His own home church? To be honest, these questions baffle me and I don't think anyone I know is wise enough to answer them.

So, back to reading 7. Jen says this:

> I'm at that place where "well done" trumps "well said." When I see kingdom work in the middle of brokenness, when mission transitions from the academic soil of the mind into the sacrificial work of someone else's hands, I am utterly affected. Obedience inspires me. Servant leaders inspire me. Humility inspires me. Talking heads dissecting apologetics stopped inspiring me a few years ago.[4]

Yes! I have reached that point myself. I want to see what your "church"—institutional or otherwise—is actually doing! Are you getting dirty in kingdom work or are you patting yourselves on the back for being so wise? Are your leaders humble, working out their salvation alongside you, or are they arrogant, assuring you their way is the best (or even only!) way? Are you spending more time talking about being the church or more time DOING what Jesus actually did?

I wonder if maybe we are asking the wrong questions, looking at all of this from the wrong perspective. Maybe, just maybe, it doesn't matter if we have all the programs and trappings and a big building or if we don't . . . maybe, and this is just me thinking aloud on my keyboard, maybe the point is what each of us are doing when we're NOT with our "church." Because if we really and truly believe the church in all its forms is supposed to be a reflection of Christ, then we need to be asking ourselves if we—all of us, the collective Church, the whole Bride of Christ—reflect Him well.

I know the language of church, I'm fluent in all the "tions"—sanctification, justification, salvation, etc. But...

> IF I SPEAK IN THE TONGUES OF MEN AND OF ANGELS,
> BUT HAVE NOT LOVE, I AM A NOISY GONG OR A
> CLANGING SYMBOL. 1 CORINTHIANS 13:1

I wonder sometimes if all our discussions about the best kind of church is just a whole lot of noise in heaven. Because when we spend more time "discussing" than "as you go"-ing (Matthew 28:19-20), my observation is that we also begin to move farther and farther from being known as He wants us to be known:

> BY **THIS** ALL PEOPLE KNOW THAT YOU ARE MY
> DISCIPLES, IF YOU HAVE LOVE FOR ONE ANOTHER.
> JOHN 13:35, EMPHASIS ADDED

This? This is love . . . and in far too many conversations about the "right" way to "do church," loving one another gets lost in "being right."

I have no idea what the best way to do church is . . . I imagine there are as many different ways to do it as there are places in which it can be done.

Prayer from the Pew:

God, it doesn't really matter to You, does it? What kind of music we sing or whether we meet in an ornate sanctuary or down by the river is never the point. You, You are the point. When we come together, this broken, messed up Body of Christ, when we enter Your presence, we are changed. When we sit in Your glory, offering You ourselves, we are transformed into this beautiful picture of You. The Body of Christ, whole and glorious, making known One Name, THE Name! Teach me to lay aside being right and relentlessly pursue being righteous. In church and out. In the name of the One who IS righteous and true, Amen.

Christ Is Proclaimed

LET YOUR RELIGION BE LESS OF A THEORY AND MORE OF A LOVE AFFAIR.

G. K. CHESTERTON

We get caught up in the crazy sometimes, don't we? The discussion and theories and programs and practices become the focus. In all of the striving to be purpose driven or radical, it's so easy to forget about Jesus. We find ourselves comparing numbers, longing to be the next "big thing." We look around our churches and begin to think if we had a preacher like him or a worship leader who could do that, THEN we'd be satisfied.

That little desire for recognition can lead to some dangerous places.

> Some indeed preach Christ from envy and rivalry, but others from good will. The latter do it out of love, knowing that I am put here for the defense of the gospel. The former proclaim Christ out of rivalry, not sincerely but thinking to afflict me in my imprisonment. What then? **Only that in every way, whether in pretense or in truth, Christ is proclaimed, and in that I rejoice.** Yes, and I will rejoice, for I know that through your prayers and the help of the Spirit of Jesus Christ this will turn out for my deliverance.
>
> Philippians 1:15-19, emphasis added

Paul's one desire was to see Christ proclaimed. He knew others were doing so out of impure motives and with wrong hearts. But he rejoiced in the fact that Christ was being preached.

So often, we in churches find ourselves dealing with jealousy and envy. Another church is growing while ours is not. Another Sunday school class is doing amazing things while ours is not. Another believer is receiving great opportunities while we are not.

Rather than celebrating that the gospel is proclaimed, we allow our hearts to become bitter and jealous. We speak out against the motives and methods, claiming superiority, but losing sight of the truth: Christ proclaimed is all that matters!

Whether the version of the Bible is KJV or NLT, whether the music is contemporary or traditional, whether the preacher wears suits or shorts, whether the church has a steeple or a coffee bar . . . when Christ is proclaimed, we must rejoice! Together.

We get distracted, don't we? By all sorts of things that really don't matter.

Sometime we forget to rejoice when His name is lifted up, no matter what. It's hard to rejoice when we're resentful.

We lack a joy that isn't jealous.

We fail to live in the truth that God's Word never returns void and His will is accomplished through ways we will never comprehend.

We need to lay down our egos and we need to echo the words of Paul, "Christ is proclaimed, and in that I rejoice."

Prayer from the Pew:

Lord, will You teach me to rejoice when Your name is proclaimed no matter what? Give me a joy for the Gospel that celebrates when another faith family experiences growth because I know the Kingdom is growing. Give me a desire to pray for other churches—even the ones who do things I don't understand—and to join with them as brothers and sisters in Christ to share the grace of salvation. Forgive me for the times when I'm petty and jealous. Create in me a longing for You that far surpasses any desire for me or my church to be recognized. In Jesus' name, Amen.

I pray to see GOD in every person. (From Stations of the cross) 4/3/15 - Good Fri, RHBC

The Necessity of Silence

> **I LIKE THE SILENT CHURCH BEFORE THE SERVICE BEGINS BETTER THAN ANY PREACHING.**
>
> RALPH WALDO EMERSON

We fear the quiet. We run from it, hiding ourselves from the secrets the silence brings. We crave the noise, leaving televisions playing all day long just to block out the empty we feel in the stillness.

Silence scares us. The lingering stillness of nothing leaves us skittish, uncertain. Our world is loud and noisy. It's what we know; it's where we feel safe. So we stay there, stay busy, stay loud. We multi-task and surround ourselves with 24-hour news and the steady beat of notifications on our cell phones.

Even in our worship, we want the noise. Oh the type of noise we want varies according to our personal tastes, but stillness is rarely a routine part of most church services.

A few years ago at a Good Friday service my husband led, the music ceased suddenly. In a room filled with people, it took less than a minute before the shifting in the seats ended the uncomfortable silence that surrounded us.

Within ninety seconds, the whispers began, "What is going on?" Before two minutes had passed, the heaviness of discomfort covered the room.

No one explained what was going on. A pastor didn't end the service with prayer. We weren't given the "You're dismissed" notification. Everything stopped.

We had no directions, no warning, no explanation. Just quiet. An appropriate ending to a Good Friday service designed to remind us of the heaviness of that day when Christ was crucified.

But even now when I think back to those moments, it is not the agony of the disciples following the crucifixion that digs deep into me. It is my own fear of the quiet.

God speaks in the quiet. He tells us it is there we know Him.

> BE STILL AND KNOW THAT I AM GOD.
> PSALM 46:10

At a conference I recently attended with my husband, author Ian Morgan Cron challenged us, "Do not speak until the silence gives consent." He was speaking in regard to leading worship and creating environments in the church setting. But what if we applied that same idea to our personal worship experiences?

What if we sat still before God waiting in anticipation before we ever uttered a word of prayer?

What if our preparation for corporate worship was private silence before the Creator?

How would our churches be changed, our prayer lives be changed, if our first inclination was stillness, silence, instead of speech?

Prayer from the Pew:

You are Creator of everything from nothing. When the earth was dark and void, You spoke. Your voice is the beginning of life. Lord, teach me that truth. Teach me to long for the silence where You alone fill the emptiness. Cause me to yearn for the solitude where You are best met. I see You in the thunder and lightning and the crashing of the waves, now will You teach me the wonders of meeting You in the gentle breeze and twilight stillnesss? Move me from the noise into the silence. In Jesus' name, Amen.

Partakers of Grace

> **GRACE IS MY FAVOURITE CHURCH WORD. A STATE OF BEING. SOMETHING YOU CAN PRAY FOR. SOMETHING GOD CAN GRANT. SOMETHING YOU CAN OBTAIN. PERFECTION IS OUT OF REACH. BUT GRACE—GRACE YOU CAN REACH FOR.**
>
> ELIZABETH SCOTT

Paul's letter to the Philippians has long been one of my favorite portions of Scripture. Four short chapters filled with such encouragement and blessing. Passages reminding us not to worry but to trust Him (Philippians 4:6). Verses challenging us to live in humility with Christ as our example (Philippians 2:5-11). So many familiar words in that little letter. And tucked away in the beginning of this epistle of joy, we find these words from the apostle:

> IT IS RIGHT FOR ME TO FEEL THIS WAY ABOUT YOU ALL, BECAUSE I HOLD YOU IN MY HEART, FOR YOU ARE ALL **PARTAKERS WITH ME OF GRACE**, BOTH IN MY IMPRISONMENT AND IN THE DEFENSE AND CONFIRMATION OF THE GOSPEL. FOR GOD IS MY WITNESS HOW I YEARN FOR YOU ALL WITH AFFECTION OF CHRIST JESUS.
>
> PHILIPPIANS 1:7-8 EMPHASIS ADDED

Are you a partaker of grace? <u>Sometimes I think we just graze at grace.</u> Rather than sitting down at the full table the Lord has offered us, we wander around nibbling at the bite-sized things we can hold in our hands.

Paul honored the Philippian church as partakers of grace—they embraced the hard, painful grace. Could the same be said of us? Do we embrace the hard grace? Or do we merely want the "sample size" grace? Just enough to feel good.

Far too often I fear we, in the American church especially, are grazing at the grace table, and we are missing the fullness that only comes from being a partaker of grace.

Will you join me on this journey of grace? Learning to pray and growing in grace are lifelong pursuits. But we must have changed hearts and opened arms for the church, this Bride of Christ. Jesus, our Bridegroom, looks at us with eager anticipation of the day He will come to take us

home. Until then, we must pursue grace and unity in His name. And that will only come as we commit ourselves to prayer.

Prayer from the Pew

Teach us, Oh Lord, to be partakers of grace. Let us not be satisfied with mere samplings of the beauty You offer but cause our hearts to long for the fullness of Your bounty. Open our hearts to love one another and give us a willing heart to accept the differences and love, above all to love. May it be said of my church, as of the church at Philippi, that we are partakers of grace. In Jesus' name, Amen.

Thirty Prayers for Your Church

PRAYER DOES NOT FIT US FOR THE GREATER WORK; PRAYER IS THE GREATER WORK.

OSWALD CHAMBERS

Prayers for the Heart of Your Church

THE TRUE CHURCH LIVES AND MOVES AND HAS ITS BEING IN PRAYER.
LEONARD RAVENHILL

Prayer for "One Heart"

AND THE CONGREGATION OF THOSE WHO BELIEVED
WERE OF ONE HEART ...
ACTS 4:32 NASB

Lord, we pray our faith fellowship will be bound with one heart—a heart that seeks You, is passionate for You, longs for You alone. As we grow in one heart for You, fill us with great love and compassion for one another as well. Cause us to lay down our own agendas, plans, and desires. Let them be replaced with humility and love that places others ahead of ourselves. May we be so consumed with loving and serving that people know it can only be explained by You. Amen.

Prayer to Be Spirit-Filled

AND THEY WERE ALL FILLED WITH THE HOLY SPIRIT ...
ACTS 4:2

Lord, we pray that Your church will be filled with the Holy Spirit. God, That We Will Be guided by the Teacher and Counselor You have sent to us. We ask that Your Spirit fill us with the fruit that only comes from You— love, joy, peace, patience, kindness, goodness, faithfulness, gentleness, and self-control. We pray that, as Your beloved Bride, we will be a radiant picture of Your love for the world around us. Keep us, O Lord, from arrogance, competition, and strife between other congregations. Cause us to walk in one mind, be of one heart, and be ever guided by one Spirit. Amen

Prayer That We Encourage One Another

AND ALL THOSE WHO HAD BELIEVED WERE TOGETHER,
AND HAD ALL THINGS IN COMMON.
ACTS 2:44

Lord, we are often guilty of focusing on our differences. Teach us to celebrate what we have in common. Reveal to us how to encourage one another with the truth of Your love, grace, and mercy that bless us all. Forgive us for the times when we belittle and judge each other, for those moments when malice or envy is our motivator. Replace those attitudes and insecurities with a love for You that spills over into a desire to support and encourage others. And, Lord, as we become encouragers to one another, we pray That We Will Be a shining light in this world. Amen.

Prayer That We Will Be Bold

FOR WE CANNOT STOP SPEAKING WHAT WE HAVE SEEN AND HEARD.
ACTS 4:20

Father, give our congregation boldness in sharing Your love with a lost, dark, and dying world. May we never be guilty of hiding the great light You have placed inside us. Rather, let us be ever focused on proclaiming the message of salvation that comes only through Jesus Christ, Your Son, our Lord. Amen.

Prayer That We Will Be Generous

For there was not a needy person among them, for all who were owners of the land or houses would sell them and bring the proceeds of the sales, and lay them at the apostles' feet; and they would be distributed to each, as any had need.
Acts 4:34-35

God, great Giver of all things, may we, Your people, be ever mindful that all we have is given by Your good pleasure and is not for our own selfish desires but for Your glory. Cause us, as individuals and as a church body, to be generous – giving sacrificially of our time, energy, and resources. Teach us to be "need meters" in the lives of others and to be joyful givers with no desire for recognition or praise here on earth. Let us never hold tightly to the things of this world, where moth and rust destroy, but instead, by continually investing in those things that are eternal, may our treasure always be other people and our hearts be led by a desire to give as freely and generously as You have given to us. Amen.

Prayer That We Will Be Honest

But a certain man named Ananias, with his wife Sapphira, sold a piece of property, and kept back some of the price for himself, with his wife's full knowledge, and bringing a portion of it, he laid it at the apostles' feet. But Peter said, "Ananias, why has Satan filled your heart to lie to the Holy Spirit, and to keep back some of the price of the land? While it remained unsold, did it not remain your own? And after it was sold, was it not under your control? Why is it that you have conceived this deed in your heart? You have not lied to men, but to God."

Acts 5:1-4

God, teach us to be upright in all things. Cause our church to be a place of integrity and truthfulness. Help us work together without deceit or malice. Fill our words and our hearts with honesty. Teach us to understand that as we deal with one another, we are dealing with You. Let us do nothing that would bring shame upon the name of Christ, and help us to live in a manner that is above reproach in all things, at all times. Amen.

Prayer That We Will Be Prepared for Persecution

AND THEY TOOK HIS ADVICE; AND AFTER CALLING THE APOSTLES IN, THEY FLOGGED THEM AND ORDERED THEM TO SPEAK NO MORE IN THE NAME OF JESUS, AND THEN RELEASED THEM. SO THEY WENT ON THEIR WAY FROM THE PRESENCE OF THE COUNCIL, <u>REJOICING THAT THEY HAD BEEN CONSIDERED WORTHY TO SUFFER SHAME FOR HIS NAME.</u> AND EVERY DAY, IN THE TEMPLE AND FROM HOUSE TO HOUSE, THEY KEPT RIGHT ON TEACHING AND PREACHING JESUS AS THE CHRIST.
ACTS 5:40-42

Lord, how often we fail to realize how truly blessed we are to worship You freely. But we are not unaware of the days ahead in which those freedoms may be stripped away. Even now, we pray You will give us a passion for You that transcends mortal explanation. A passion that will keep us steadfast and focused as the pressures and persecution against Your church rise. Cause us to be bold and true to Your Word and prepare us to face the days ahead with courage and zeal for You. Amen.

Prayer That We Will Be Committed to the Word

BUT SELECT FROM AMONG YOU, BRETHREN, SEVEN MEN OF GOOD REPUTATION, FULL OF THE SPIRIT AND OF WISDOM, WHOM WE MAY PUT IN CHARGE OF THIS TASK. BUT WE WILL DEVOTE OURSELVES TO PRAYER, AND TO THE MINISTRY OF THE WORD.
ACTS 6:3-4

Father, give us hearts that are committed to DOING. We realize what we hear and learn on Sundays must be evident in our lives Monday through Saturday. <u>Cause us to be a church that seeks obedience to Your Word</u>, that we will submit ourselves to Scripture. We pray You will do a might work AMONG us, IN us, and THROUGH us. We long to be motivated to serve and set aside the idea that the work of ministry will be done by those who are paid staff in our church. Cause each of us to be faithful to DO and as we are obedient, we pray others will be drawn to Your great love. Amen.

Prayer That We Will Be Grace-Filled (part 1)

But Ananias answered, "Lord, I have heard from many about this man, how much evil he has done to your saints in Jerusalem. And here he has authority from the chief priest to bind all who call on your name." But the Lord said to him, "Go, for he is a chosen instrument of mine to carry my name before the Gentiles and kinds and the children of Israel. <u>For I will show him how much he must suffer for the sake of my name.</u>" So Ananias departed and entered the house. And laying his hands on him he said, "Brother Saul, the Lord Jesus who appeared to you on the road by which you came has sent me so that you may regain your sight and be filled with the Holy Spirit."
Acts 9:13-17

Father, forgive us for the way we accept the grace You so generously give and then fail to believe that others can be changed by Your love and mercy. Teach us to trust the change You bring into the lives of those who belong to You. Cause us to have the heart of obedience and faith that Ananias had as he went to Saul, believing that You can and do change the hearts of people completely. Protect us from being caught up in our own prejudice or small-mindedness but to always view others through the lens of Your grace. Amen.

Prayer That We Will Be Grace-Filled (part 2)

AND HE SAID TO THEM, "YOU YOURSELVES KNOW HOW UNLAWFUL IT IS FOR A MAN WHO IS A JEW TO ASSOCIATE WITH A FOREIGNER OR TO VISIT HIM; AND YET GOD HAS SHOWN ME THAT I SHOULD NOT CALL ANY MAN UNHOLY OR UNCLEAN."
ACTS 10:28

<u>Lord, we pray that we will not be caught up in the chains of legalism, of judging one another.</u> Cause us to be filled with grace and be willing to accept other and extend mercy. We know the destruction legalism can bring and we pray our church will ever be on guard against such things. Protect us and give us wisdom as we seek to follow You. Amen.

Prayers for the Ministry of Your Church

THERE HAS NEVER BEEN A SPIRITUAL AWAKENING IN ANY COUNTRY OR LOCALITY THAT DID NOT BEGIN IN UNITED PRAYER.

A. T. PIERSON

Prayer for Christ-Centeredness in the Church

THEREFORE LET ALL THE HOUSE OF ISRAEL KNOW FOR CERTAIN THAT GOD HAS MADE HIM BOTH LORD AND CHRIST—THIS JESUS WHOM YOU CRUCIFIED.
ACTS 2:36

Father, we come humbly before You grateful for the gift of Your beloved Son. May we, as the Body of Christ, never forget the great sacrifice He has made for our salvation. Teach us to keep Him at the core of all we do—preaching and teaching Christ crucified and raised again, the only way to relationship with You. <u>Draw us away from the snare and distractions of the enemy and keep us focused on proclaiming the mercy, grace, and love You have so generously offered to us.</u> In all things, we pray for Your heart, Your mind. Fill us with a passionate desire to see "Your will be done, on earth as it is in Heaven." Amen.

Prayer for Continual Bible Teaching in the Church

AND THEY WERE CONTINUALLY DEVOTING THEMSELVES TO THE APOSTLES' TEACHING AND TO FELLOWSHIP, TO THE BREAKING OF BREAD AND TO PRAYER.
ACTS 2:42

Holy God, we long to be passionate about Your Word. Fill our places of worship with urgency for the Bible. <u>Cause our small groups to be focused on biblical wisdom not man's words. Fill our pulpits with those who will unashamedly proclaim the Word of God.</u> Grant us wisdom to base every ministry of our church on the foundation of Your Word. But God, we also pray we will never merely be "hearers of the Word" but that we will put what You reveal into action in our lives. We pray that as we are devoted to Your Word, You will use us and people will say, "I've never seen it like that before." Amen.

Prayer That We Will Be Fellowship Seeking

AND THEY WERE CONTINUALLY DEVOTING THEMSELVES TO THE APOSTLES' TEACHING AND TO FELLOWSHIP, TO THE BREAKING OF BREAD AND TO PRAYER.
ACTS 2:42

Lord, teach us to love one another. Not just to say it; but to do it, to live it. Show us that "more excellent way" that is true, unselfish love. Help us to delight in one another's company and to build strong relationships with each other. Cause us to understand that fellowship with others is another way of enjoying fellowship with You. Help us to grasp the significance of time spent together, of building relationships, of sharing joy and sorrow, and of doing ministry in Your name. Lord, may our churches be places where love for others is abundant. Amen.

Prayer That We Will Be Devoted to Prayer

AND THEY WERE CONTINUALLY DEVOTING THEMSELVES TO THE APOSTLES' TEACHING AND TO FELLOWSHIP, TO THE BREAKING OF BREAD AND TO PRAYER.
ACTS 2:42

Oh Father, how often we are guilty of neglecting this most important thing, of communicating with You. We spend our time in church listening to one another and fail to join together to listen to You. Forgive us for allowing Your house to be anything but a "House of Prayer." Change us, Lord, and fill us with a desire to pray. Cause us to grasp the power of prayer and to realize our need for prayer. Fill us will a desire to seek You before we do anything else. Give us a longing to be devoted to prayer. Amen.

Prayer That We Will Be Known for Praising God

(THEY WERE) PRAISING GOD, AND HAVING FAVOR WITH ALL THE PEOPLE . . .
ACTS 2:47

Father give our church a love for You that is honest and expressed at all times in praise of Your great love. Christ said that if He were lifted up, He would draw men to You. We pray that we will continually lift the name and praise of Jesus Christ, our Lord and Savior. May we never be guilty of offering our praise to one another or to an other idol, but only to Christ, the name that is above all names. Teach us to worship in spirit and in truth so those who do not know You will be drawn in to relationship with You. We pray all we do is focused on glorifying You and never on brining attention to ourselves. Cause us, in all things—whether good or bad, whether we understand or not—to give all praise to Your name. Amen.

Prayer That We Will Be Blessed by Growth

AND THE LORD WAS ADDING TO THEIR NUMBER DAY BY DAY THOSE WHO WERE BEING SAVED.
ACTS 2:47

God, we pray for growth in our churches. We pray for those who live in darkness to find the light You offer through salvation. We long to see our sanctuaries and classrooms full. We want to see You change lives, restore families, and renew hope. We don't ask for growth for its own sake or for ours, but only growth that will glorify You. We ask that YOU add to our number and we pray we will always be humble and recognize it is You at work, not us or our programs. Fill us with a longing to share Your love and merciful salvation at all times. We pray the Holy Spirit will work through us to draw others to You. We praise You for the sweetest truth that You desire "none would perish but all would have eternal life." <u>Fill us with faithfulness to the Great Commission, that we would tell of You as we go</u>. Amen.

Prayer That We Will Be Gospel Focused

NEVERTHELESS, MORE AND MORE MEN AND WOMEN BELIEVED IN THE LORD AND WERE ADDED TO THEIR NUMBER.
ACTS 5:14 NIV

Lord, may we be devoted to seeking opportunities to share of Your great love. How we pray that we will never be guilty of letting the "nevertheless" stop us from seeking Kingdom growth. Give us eyes that see those in need around us and hearts that long to share truth, freedom, mercy, and grace. Use us, Lord, in our homes, in our schools, in our workplaces, in the grocery store, at the park. <u>AS WE GO</u> cause us to be disciple-makers, always prepared to give an account of the great gift of salvation through Jesus Christ our Lord. Amen.

Prayer That We Will Be Faithful to Send

AND WHEN THEY WERE MINISTERING TO THE LORD AND FASTING, THE HOLY SPIRIT SAID, "SET APART FOR ME BARNABAS AND SAUL FOR THE WORK TO WHICH I HAVE CALLED THEM." THEN, WHEN THEY HAD FASTED AND PRAYED AND LAID THEIR HANDS ON THEM, THEY SENT THEM AWAY.
ACTS 13:2-3

Lord, we ask for an urgent desire in our church to send out others. Cause us to be faithful to reaching beyond our doors, to encouraging others in mission endeavors, and to be willing to sacrifice whatever is necessary to spread the Good News. Let us never be guilty of hoarding the message of salvation within our doors but give us a passion for sharing the Gospel. Amen.

Prayers for Your Pastors

IF THE CHURCH WANTS A BETTER PASTOR, IT NEEDS ONLY TO PRAY FOR THE ONE IT HAS.

UNKNOWN

Prayer That Your Pastors Will Boldly Proclaim the Word

Then Peter, filled with the Holy Spirit, said to them, "Rulers and elders of the people, if we are on trial today for a benefit done to a sick man, as to how this man has been made well, let it be known to all of you and to all the people of Israel, that by the name of Jesus Christ the Nazarene, whom you crucified, whom God raised from the dead—by this name this man stands here before you in good health. He is the stone which was rejected by you the builders, but which became the very corner stone. And there is salvation in no one else; for there is no other name under heaven that has been given among men, by which we must be saved."

Acts 4:8-12

Lord, we pray for our pastors. We ask that they be bold in their proclamation of the Good News. We pray they have courage and wisdom to know what to say and how to say it. We ask that they be Spirit-filled and faithful to the calling You have placed on their lives. Thank You, God, for the pastors You have given to our churches. Cause us to be faithful to honor You through our treatment of them. Amen.

Prayer That Your Pastors Will Seek God Alone

But Peter and John answered and said to them, "Whether it is right in the sight of God to give heed to you rather than to God, you be the judge; for we cannot stop speaking what we have seen and heard."
Acts 4:19-20

Father, we ask that You fill our pastors with a fervent desire to please You, that their hearts' longing will be obedience to You above all things. We ask that You protect their minds from the trappings of this world and from those who would seek to shift their focus away from You. We pray that You guide them daily in all things—from smallest to largest—and that You continually whisper Your great love for them to their hearts. We know the demands on their time and energy are great, and we pray they will not be distracted from You. Draw our pastors close to You. We pray in all things they will truly find You are sufficient. Amen.

Prayer That Your Pastors Will Be Devoted to Prayer

BUT WE WILL DEVOTE OURSELVES TO PRAYER, AND TO THE MINISTRY OF THE WORD.
ACTS 6:4

Lord, we pray that our pastors will keep their focus on prayer in all things, recognizing the great privilege and responsibility they have to shepherd the flock and proclaim the Word. We realize without adequate prayer, they cannot do what You have called them to do. Cause us to be supportive of that calling in their lives and to be willing always to step up and do what is necessary to afford them adequate time for prayer and study. But most of all, we pray that our pastors will have an insatiable need for time with You. Amen.

Prayer That Your Pastors Will Be Committed to the Word

BUT WE WILL DEVOTE OURSELVES TO PRAYER, AND TO THE MINISTRY OF THE WORD.
ACTS 6:4

Father, we lift up our pastors to You, asking for Your protection of their bodies, minds, and spirits. We know the attacks against them and their families are great. We ask that You give them a passion for Your Word and a yearning to spend time growing in their understanding of Scripture. Reveal Yourself to them through their study. We pray they will be committed to preparation of their sermons and seek the Holy Spirit's guidance early for direction. We thank You for pastors who are excellent speakers, but we pray they will never have confidence in their abilities to communicate and thus neglect giving time to study and prayer. As You speak to our pastors, use them to challenge us. Amen.

Praying for Yourself and Fellow Believers

OF ALL THE DUTIES ENJOINED BY CHRISTIANITY NONE IS MORE ESSENTIAL AND YET MORE NEGLECTED THAN PRAYER.

FRANCOIS FÉNELON

Prayer for Healing— Physical, Emotional, Mental, Spiritual

AND ALSO THE PEOPLE FROM THE CITIES IN THE VICINITY OF JERUSALEM WERE COMING TOGETHER, BRINGING PEOPLE WHO WERE SICK OR AFFLICTED WITH UNCLEAN SPIRITS; AND THEY WERE ALL BEING HEALED.
ACTS 5:16

God, may we seek healing from You in our lives and in the lives of those in our church. Free us from those things that bind us, that make us less than whole. Teach us to understand true healing from You, that makes us well though we face sickness. Give us grace to deal with life's sufferings but fill us with the strength and peace to keep our focus on You. Cause our church to be a place of healing, where the broken and hurting find love, comfort, and acceptance. Use us, Lord, as a hospital for those in pain. We long to live in the healing only You can provide and to share that healing with others. Amen.

Prayer That We Be Filled with Grace

AND STEPHEN, FULL OF GRACE AND POWER, WAS PERFORMING GREAT WONDERS AND SIGNS AMONG THE PEOPLE.
ACTS 6:8

Lord, may we as believers be like Stephen, filled with Your grace and power, able to do mighty things in Your name as a result of our faith in You. May we extend the grace we have received to those around us as an example of Your mercy. Help us always to remember our own need for grace and keep us humble. Amen.

Prayer That We Will Be Forgiving

AND THEY WENT ON STONING STEPHEN AS HE CALLED UPON THE LORD AND SAID, "LORD JESUS, RECEIVE MY SPIRIT!" AND FALLING ON HIS KNEES, HE CRIED OUT WITH A LOUD VOICE, "LORD, DO NOT HOLD THIS SIN AGAINST THEM!" AND HAVING SAID THIS, HE FELL ASLEEP.
ACTS 7:59-60

Father, we pray we will have the humility and grace of Stephen, who faced his death in Your name with grace and forgiveness for those who wronged him. Forgive us of the times we fail to forgive others, for the grudges we harbor, the ill we bear. Instead, give us eyes that see as You see. Open our hearts to people in need of love and mercy. Cause us to let go of the pride that wants to be right and give instead tenderness and compassion for those who need You. Amen.

Prayer That We Would Be "Little Christs"

AND IT CAME ABOUT THAT FOR AN ENTIRE YEAR THEY MET WITH THE CHURCH, AND TAUGHT CONSIDERABLE NUMBERS; AND THE DISCIPLES WERE FIRST CALLED CHRISTIANS AT ANTIOCH.
ACTS 11:26

Lord, teach us to walk worthy of bearing Your name—Christian, little Christ. Keep our hearts focused on You and guard us from the distractions of this world. May our lives be marked by the grace and love You have so freely given, and cause us to be extenders of the compassion You have given us. We pray we will live in a manner that reflects You and gives glory to You. Amen.

Prayer That We Would Mentor Others

And he came also to Derbe and to Lystra. And behold, a certain disciple was there, named Timothy, the son of a Jewish woman who was a believer, but his father was Greek, and he was well spoken of by the brethren who were in Lystra and Iconium. Paul wanted this man to go with him; and he took him and circumcised him because of the Jews who were in those parts, for they all knew that his father was a Greek.
Acts 16:1-3

Father, we pray for hearts that desire to invest in the lives of others. May we be like Paul, constantly seeking those who we can pour ourselves into. Help us be willing to share the journey with others, to be an encouragement and support to new believers, and to share the wisdom You so generously give to us as we help others grow in their relationships with You. Amen.

Prayer That We Will Be Prepared to Share

"As I was on my way and drew near to Damascus, about noon a great light from heaven suddenly shone around me. And I fell to the ground and heard a voice saying to me, 'Saul, Saul, why are you persecuting me?' And I answered, 'Who are you, Lord?' And he said to me, 'I am Jesus of Nazareth, whom you are persecuting.' Now those who were with me saw the light but did not understand the voice of the one who was speaking to me. And I said, 'What shall I do, Lord?' And the Lord said to me, 'Rise, and go into Damascus, and there you will be told all that is appointed for you to do.'"
Acts 22:6-10

God, we see the faith of Paul as he proclaimed his salvation story. We pray we also will have such boldness and zeal to share our faith in Christ with others. May we have courage and confidence, not in ourselves, but in You. Strengthen us to take a stand and be ready at all times to give testimony to the transforming work You have done in our lives. Amen.

Prayer That We Will Not Fear Life's Storms

AND YET NOW I URGE YOU TO KEEP UP YOUR COURAGE, FOR THERE SHALL BE NO LOSS OF LIFE AMONG YOU, BUT ONLY OF THE SHIP. FOR THIS VERY NIGHT AN ANGEL OF THE GOD TO WHOM I BELONG AND WHOM I SERVE STOOD BEFORE ME SAYING, "DO NOT BE AFRAID, PAUL; YOU MUST STAND BEFORE CAESAR; AND BEHOLD, GOD HAS GRANTED YOU ALL THOSE WHO ARE SAILING WITH YOU." THEREFORE KEEP UP YOUR COURAGE, MEN, FOR I BELIEVE GOD, THAT IT WILL TURN OUT EXACTLY AS I HAVE BEEN TOLD.
ACTS 27:22-25

Father, help us to remember You are the God of the storms and You never lose sight of us. When the winds howl around us and we fear that all is lost, draw us into Your safe presence and give us the inexplicable peace only You can provide. Amen.

The Acts of the Apostles

FORTY-DAY READING PLAN

The early church's story is powerful! Perhaps you haven't read it in awhile or maybe you've never spent time just contemplating the persecution and the enthusiasm of these first followers of The Way (Acts 19:23).

A few years ago my husband and I went on a mission trip to Roatan, Honduras. We were overwhelmed by the authenticity and expressiveness in worship of the believers we met there. Perhaps it was the lack of "extras"—like air conditioning—that lent them a perspective we in the American church often miss.

I hope by this point in reading this book, you realize how much being a part of a local faith family means to me. I'm enormously thankful to be a part of a vibrant, Bible-teaching, missions-driven church. But my church isn't perfect—no church is. And sometimes I think we all lose sight of the simple beauty of being Christians, "little Christs." I believe time spent reading the accounts of these first believers will reignite our passion for spreading the Gospel, loving one another, and serving the Lord with humility.

Next you will find a 40-day plan for reading Acts. However, there are only 38 days of readings listed because I know how life is, and it's okay if you miss a day or two. You can still finish reading these powerful 28 chapters in 40 days.

40 Day Reading Plan

Day 1	Acts 1:1 – 26
Day 2	Acts 2:1 – 36
Day 3	Acts 2:37 – 3:10
Day 4	Acts 3:11 – 4:12
Day 5	Acts 4:13 – 37
Day 6	Acts 5:1 – 32
Day 7	Acts 5:33 – 6:15
Day 8	Acts 7:1 – 40
Day 9	Acts 7:41 – 8:3
Day 10	Acts 8:4 – 40
Day 11	Acts 9:1 – 31
Day 12	Acts 9:32 – 10:22
Day 13	Acts 10:23 – 48
Day 14	Acts 11:1 – 30
Day 15	Acts 12:1 – 25
Day 16	Acts 13:1 – 28
Day 17	Acts 13:29 – 52
Day 18	Acts 14:1 – 29
Day 19	Acts 15:1 – 29
Day 20	Acts 15:30 – 16:21
Day 21	Acts 16:22 – 40
Day 22	Acts 17:1 – 21
Day 23	Acts 17:22 – 18:22
Day 24	Acts 18:23 – 19:20
Day 25	Acts 19:21 – 41
Day 26	Acts 20:1 – 27
Day 27	Acts 20:28 – 21:14

Day 28	Acts 21:15 – 40
Day 29	Acts 22:1 – 21
Day 30	Acts 22: 22 – 23:11
Day 31	Acts 23:12 – 35
Day 32	Acts 24:1 – 22
Day 33	Acts 25:1 – 22
Day 34	Acts 25:23 – 26:18
Day 35	Acts 26:19 – 27:13
Day 36	Acts 27:14 – 44
Day 37	Acts 28:1 – 15
Day 38	Acts 28:16 - 31

Discussion Questions

WHY PRAY?

What do your prayers for your church typically involve?

How do you anticipate praying for your church will change you?

I'M JUST NOT SURE ABOUT THE CHURCH SOMETIMES

Consider the Hudson Taylor quote from the beginning of this chapter. What would it require for you to devote ten days to waiting for the Spirit's power to be manifested in your church?

Do you agree or disagree with the suggestion that we are asking the wrong questions about the church? Why?

How have you observed a "me-centered" culture in your church?

THE WEAKEST LINK

Can you identify situations in which you have been the problem in your church? How does realizing this affect your relationships within the Body?

"Wounded people wound people." Discuss how you have seen this evidenced in your faith family.

RE-LIFE

What does the idea of *anazao*—recovering life—mean to your understanding of church?

How have you seen churches try to initiate revival outside the Word of God? Why is this not true revival?

The Perfect Church

What would your perfect church entail?

Discuss this statement: "My church can never be what God has called me to be."

The Problem with Church

Have you ever been ready to walk away from church? What precipitated that desire?

Why is personal humility a key factor in helping us remain connected to the body?

Well Done or Well Said

Reread the quote from Jen Hatmaker in this chapter. What is your response to her statement that well done trumps well said?

How would you respond to the idea that all (or at least a lot) of our discussions about the best kind of church is just a lot of noise in heaven?

CHRIST IS PROCLAIMED

How can we put into action G. K. Chesterton's quote, "Let your religion be less of a theory and more of a love affair"?

What has been a distraction to you in keeping focused on Christ being proclaimed?

THE NECESSITY OF SILENCE

How do you respond to silence in worship?

Discuss the quote from Ian Morgan Cron, "Do not speak until the silence gives consent" in the context of both corporate and personal worship experiences.

Partakers of Grace

How have you been guilty of grazing at grace?

What does it mean to embrace the "hard grace"?

Notes

1. James 5:16
2. http://www.bibleword.org/revival.html
3. Hebrews 12:1
4. Hatmaker, Jen, *7: An Experimental Mutiny against Excess* (Nashville: B & H Publishing Group, 2012), Kindle location 563.

Acknowledgements

BLYTHE ISLAND BAPTIST CHURCH: For almost 11 years, we served beside you all in southeast Georgia. Leaving our home there was the most difficult thing I've ever done. Thank you for letting me spend my 30s learning how to serve and love and minister among you . . . and for never giving up on me. Much of what I love most about church is the result of our time spent at BIBC.

CALVARY BAPTIST CHURCH: It's been just over a year since Scott was called as your Minister of Music. My how time flies when you're having fun! I'm thankful beyond words to be a part of this faith family. Your encouragement and support of my ministry is pure gift to me. Looking forward to all God will do as we seek His face together!

FIRST BAPTIST CHURCH, PALMYRA: What can I say to the church that God used to re-cover me with His grace and love? I came there broken and wounded. Your acceptance was balm to my heart and your love was instrumental in moving me to where I am today.

SANDRA PEOPLES: My editor, fellow pastor's wife, and soul-sister, thank you for investing in this project and for loving me well. That you are in my life is one of the richest blessings the online world has given me

ERIN ULRICH: You're my boss and one of my wisest friends. Thank you for believing in me and my message. And for helping me make it look good. Where would I be without you?

MOMMA AND DADDY: For believing in every dream I could dream up, for encouraging every passion I've displayed, and for loving me through every success and failure—thank you.

CASIDAY HOPE: You, sweet girl, are the biggest joy in my life! I know I say it all the time, but here it is again: being your mom is awesome! I'm so glad God chose me for you. I love you.

SCOTT: Sometimes words fail me. There are none sufficient to express how much I love you and how much your faith in me has changed my belief in myself. You are the best part of me and I'm so glad you listened when I told you we were supposed to get married. I love you always.

AND MOST OF ALL, JESUS: For saving me, for loving me, for molding me, for accepting me, for moving me, thank you. My only hope is that these words cause others to see You and Your love more clearly.

About the Author

Teri Lynne Underwood delights in finding glimpses of holy in the most mundane places and considers herself a purveyor of information for those seeking life where sacred and secular collide. Passionate about communicating well our responsibility to meet the needs of others, Teri Lynne loves sharing ways we can engage our world with the message of hope.

Making her home in North Alabama with her worship-leader husband, her growing-up-too-fast daughter, and her lazy-beyond-words Basset hound, Teri Lynne writes a faith column for her local paper, teaches Bible studies in her church, and reads lots of books while sitting in the car line.

She writes (almost) daily on her blog and would love to connect with you and hear your stories of grace and hope.

Website: www.terilynneu.com
Facebook: TeriLynneUBlog
Twitter: @TeriLynneU

Made in the USA
Lexington, KY
12 March 2015